ERIK SATIE

SELECTED PIANO WORKS

GNOSSIENNES
GYMNOPEDIES
SARABANDES

edited
by
WARREN THOMSON

CONTENTS

INTRODUCTION

The French composer, Erik Satie (1866-1925) was an exponent of several important trends in twentieth century composition – namely, bitonality, polytonality, jazz and harmony not based on triads.

The works in this volume are all from his earliest period of composition. At this time he also worked as a café pianist in Montmartre and studied medievalism and hence also a study of plainsong. In 1905 he entered the Schola Cantorum and studied counterpoint with Vincent D'Indy and Albert Roussel — graduating with a diploma marked 'très bien'.

During the First World War he became acquainted with Cocteau, Diaghilev and Picasso.

In the three Sarabandes we see his use of unresolved 7th and 9th chords — and these could be seen as anticipating the use of these chords in a static manner by Debussy. Satie's use of these chords however, is closely related to the melodic line(s), unlike Debussy.

Satie wrote frequently in groups of three — often each makes use of very similar material. The three Gymnopedies are his best known compositions and were probably inspired by decorations on a Greek vase. Gymnopedia was an annual festival in honour of those who died at Thyrea. These dances may represent stately dances done before statues of the gods.

The three Gnossiennes were inspired by the great palaces at Knossos on the Island of Crete which were built around 2000 B.C. and excavated between 1900-1905 after a trial excavation in 1878. In these pieces he discarded bar lines — but not for the first time. The humorous indications however, are included in these works for the first time and translations are provided here, together with some more usual French terms.

Satie's last piano works were five Nocturnes (a sixth was planned) and in these he returned to pure music.

Tempo indications and pedal markings are editorial.

Terms

ralentir — becoming slower
diminuer — getting softer
douloureux — sadly, sorrowful
triste — sadly
Très luisant — very brightly
Questionnez — ask
Du bout de la pensée — on the brink of an idea
Postulez en vous-même — make your own demands
Pas à Pas — little by little
Sur la langue — on the tip of the tongue
Avec étonnement — with astonishment
Ne sortez pas — don't leave
Dans une grande bonté — with much kindness

Plus intiment — more intimately
Avec une légere intimité — with a light intimacy
Sans orgveil — without arrogance
Conseillez-vous soigneusement — plan with care
Munissez-vous de clairvoyance — arm yourself sharply
Seul, pendant un instant — alone, for a moment
De manière à obtenir un creux — how to achieve absolutely nothing
Très perdu — quite lost
Portez cela plus loin — pursue this further
Ouvrez la tête — open your head
Enfouissez le son — muffle the sound

WARREN THOMSON

Trois Gnossiennes

à Roland Manuel
(1890)

No. I

Erik Satie

Lent (♩ = 96)

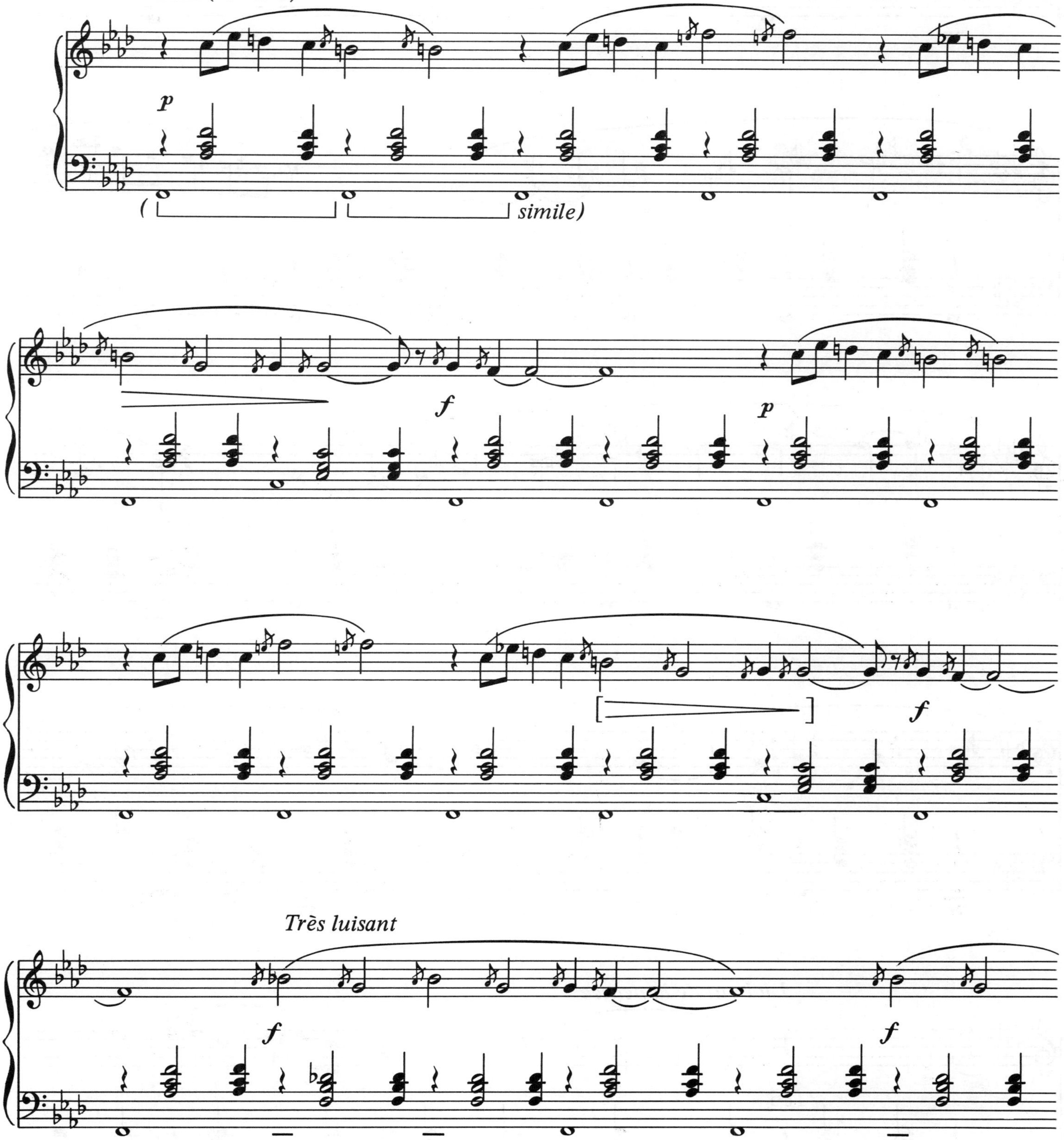

Questionnez

Du bout de la pensée

Postulez en vous-même

Pas à Pas

Sur la langue

Gnossienne
(1890)
No. II

Erik Satie

Avec étonnement (♩ = 96)

Ne sortez pas

Dans une grande bonté

Plus intimement

Avec une légere intimité

Sans orgueil

pp

Gnossienne
(1890)
No. III

Erik Satie

Lent (♩ = 84)

p

(⌐_____⌐_____*simile*)

Conseillez-vous soigneusement

Munissez-vous de clairvoyance

Seul, pendant un instant

De manière à obtenir un creux

Très perdu

Portez cela plus loin

Ouvrez la tête

Enfouissez le son

Trois Gymnopédies

à Mademoiselle Jeanne de Bret
(1888)

No. I

Erik Satie

Lent et douloureux (♩ = 88)

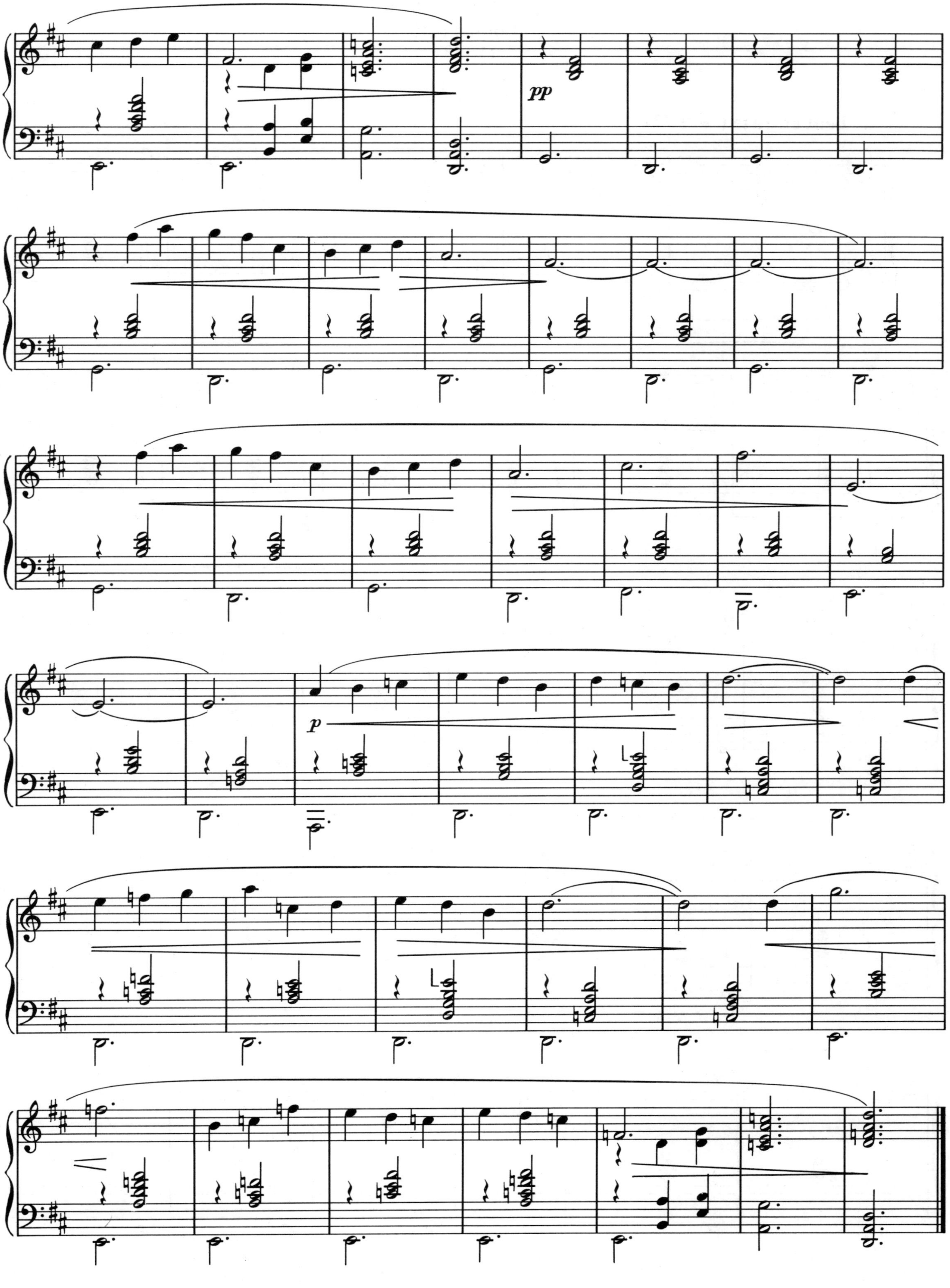
pp
p

Gymnopédie
à Conrad Satie
(1888)
No. II

Erik Satie

Lent et triste (♩ = 92)

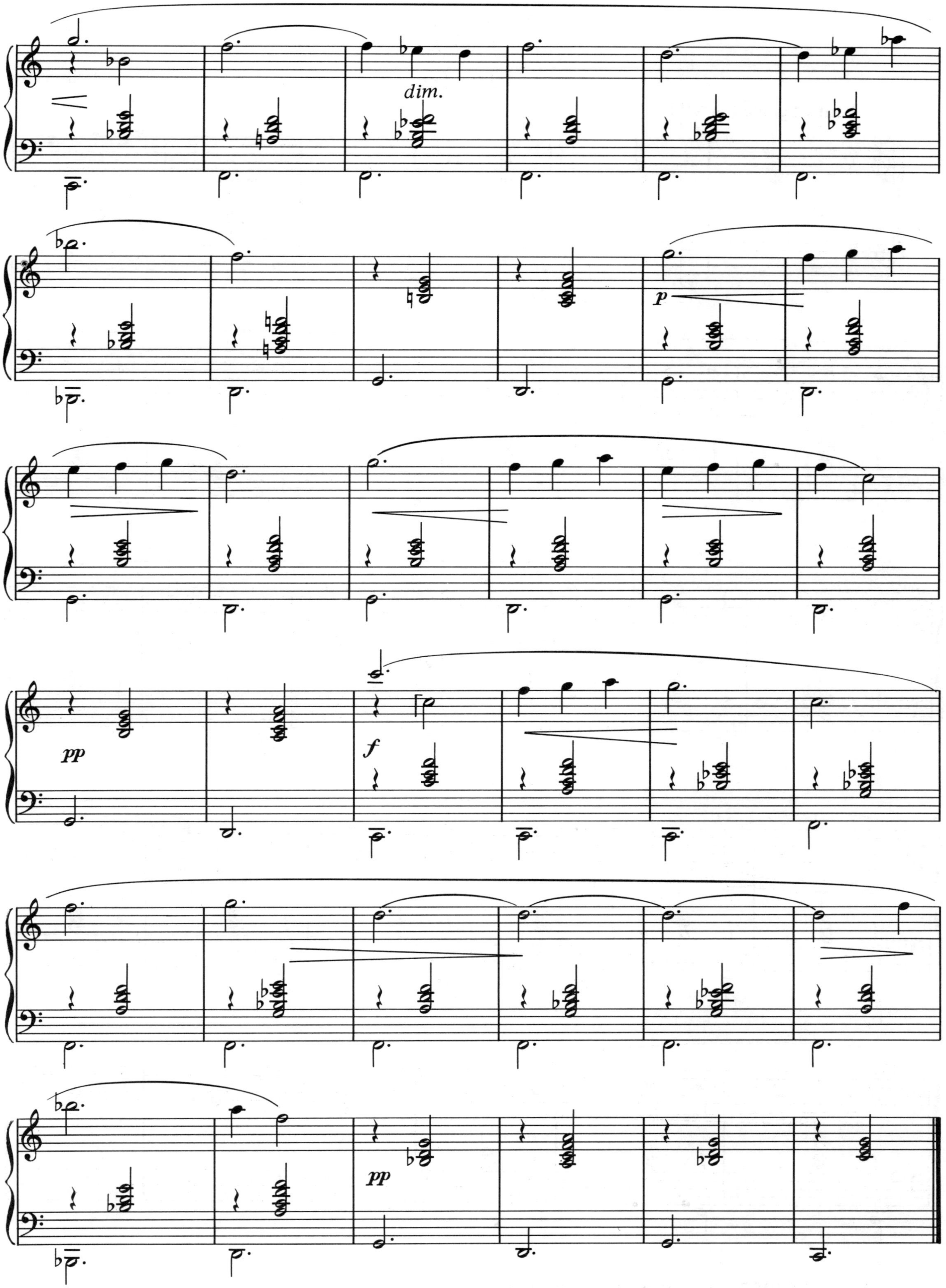
dim.
p
pp
f
pp

Gymnopédie
à Charles Levadé
(1888)

No. III

Erik Satie

Lent et grave (♩ = 92)

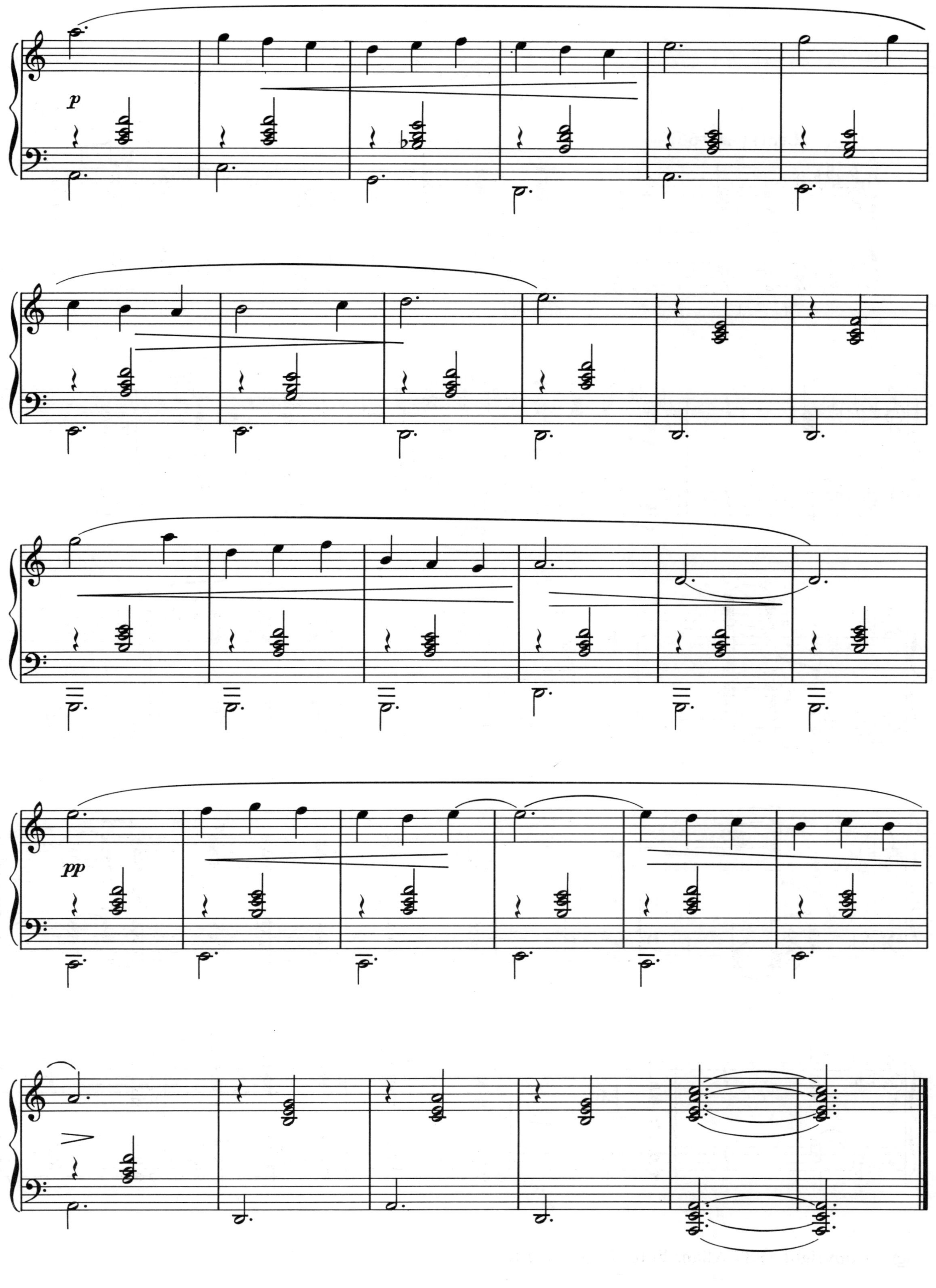
p
pp

Trois Sarabandes

(1887)

No. I

Erik Satie

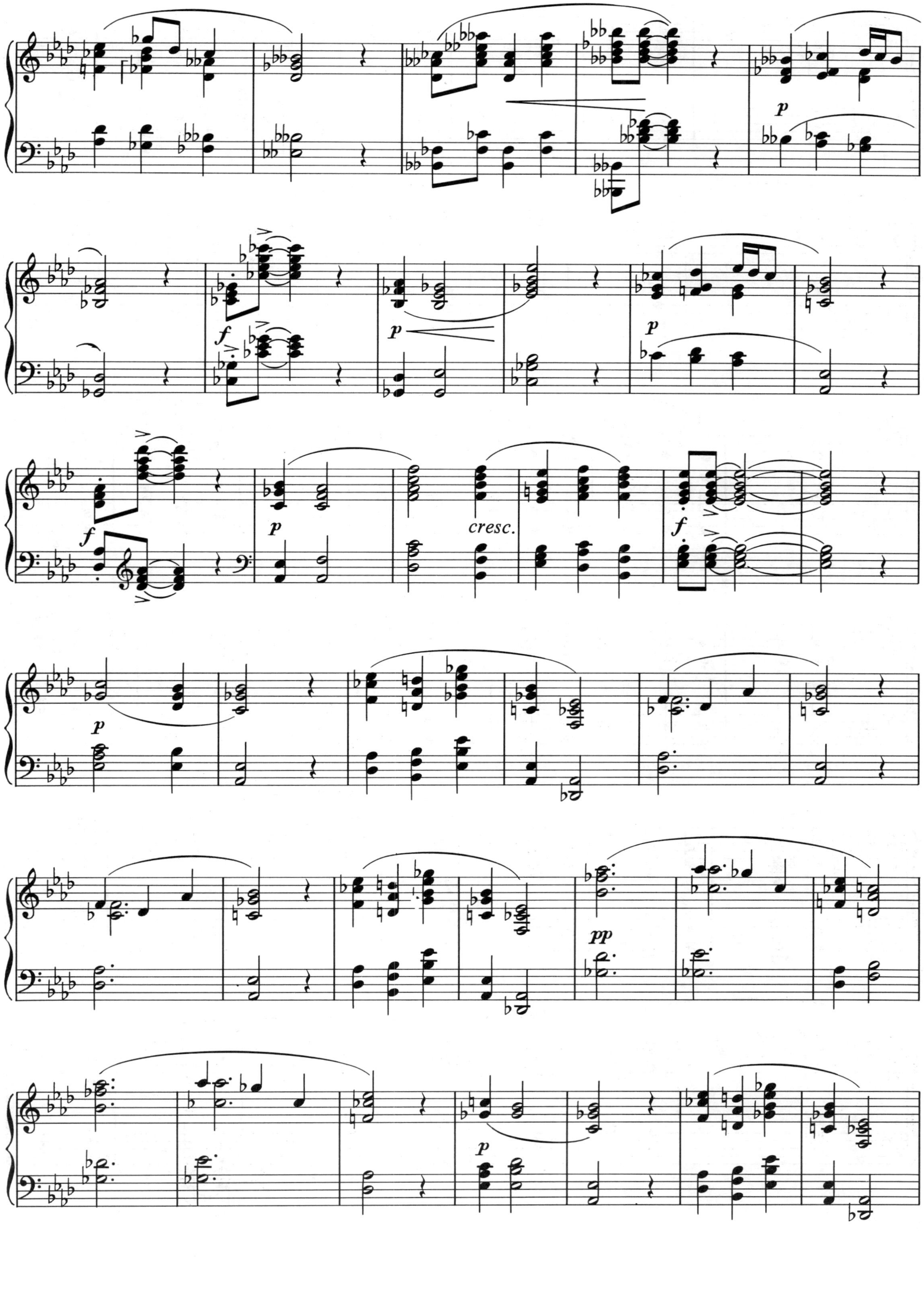
cresc.

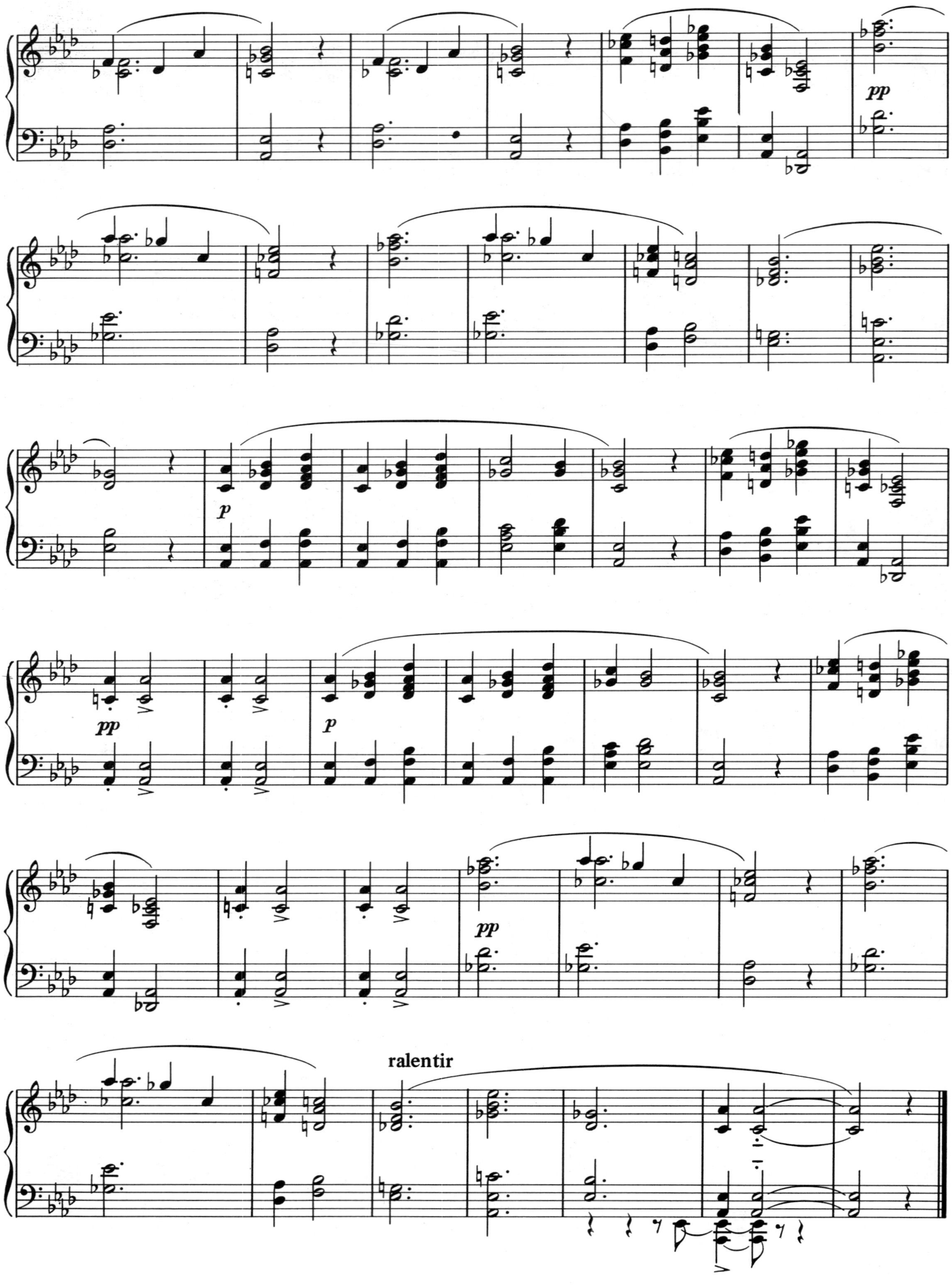
pp
p
pp
p
pp
ralentir

Sarabande
à Maurice Ravel
(1887)
No. II

Erik Satie

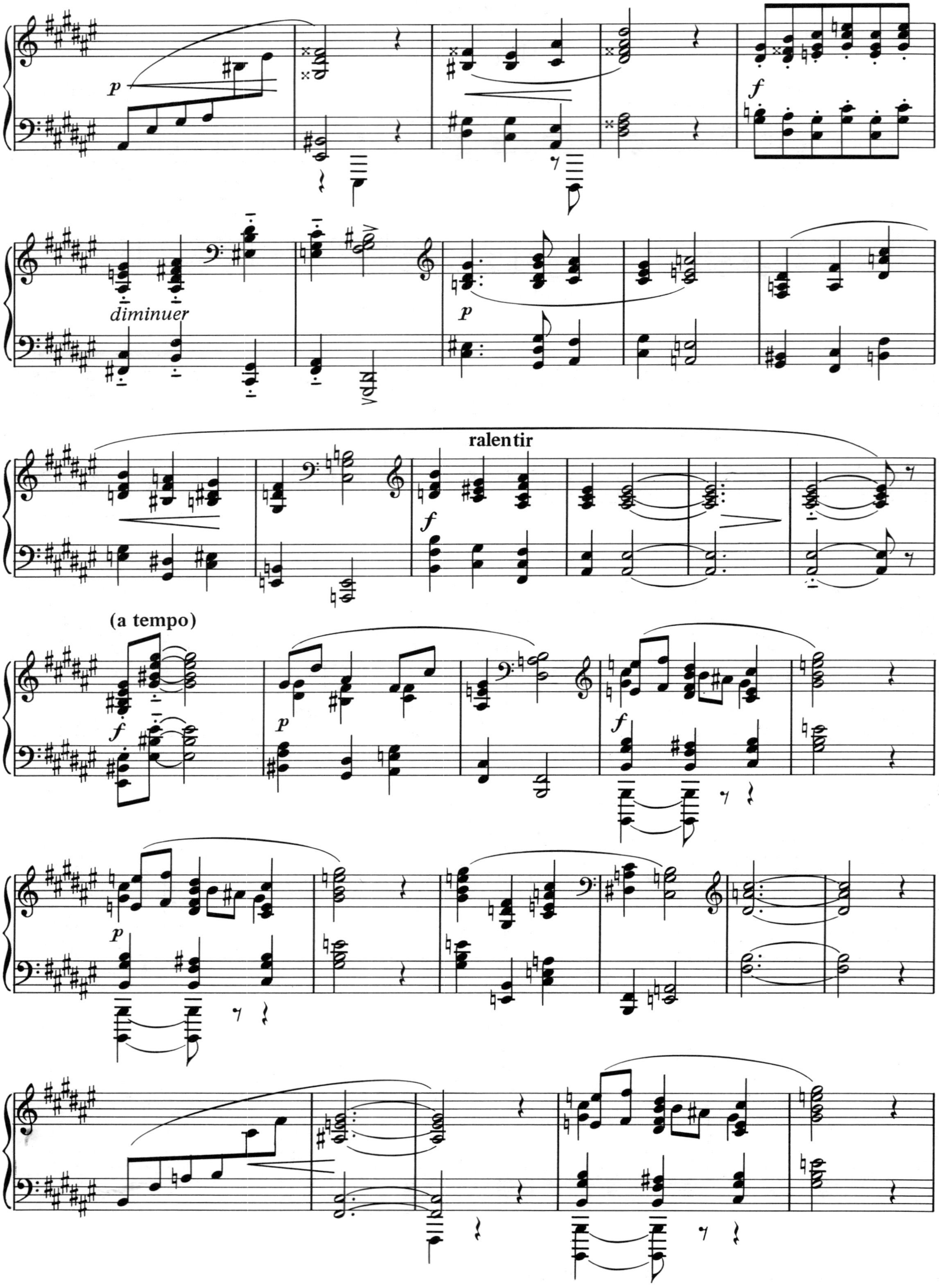
p
f
diminuer
p
ralentir
f
(a tempo)
f
p
f
p

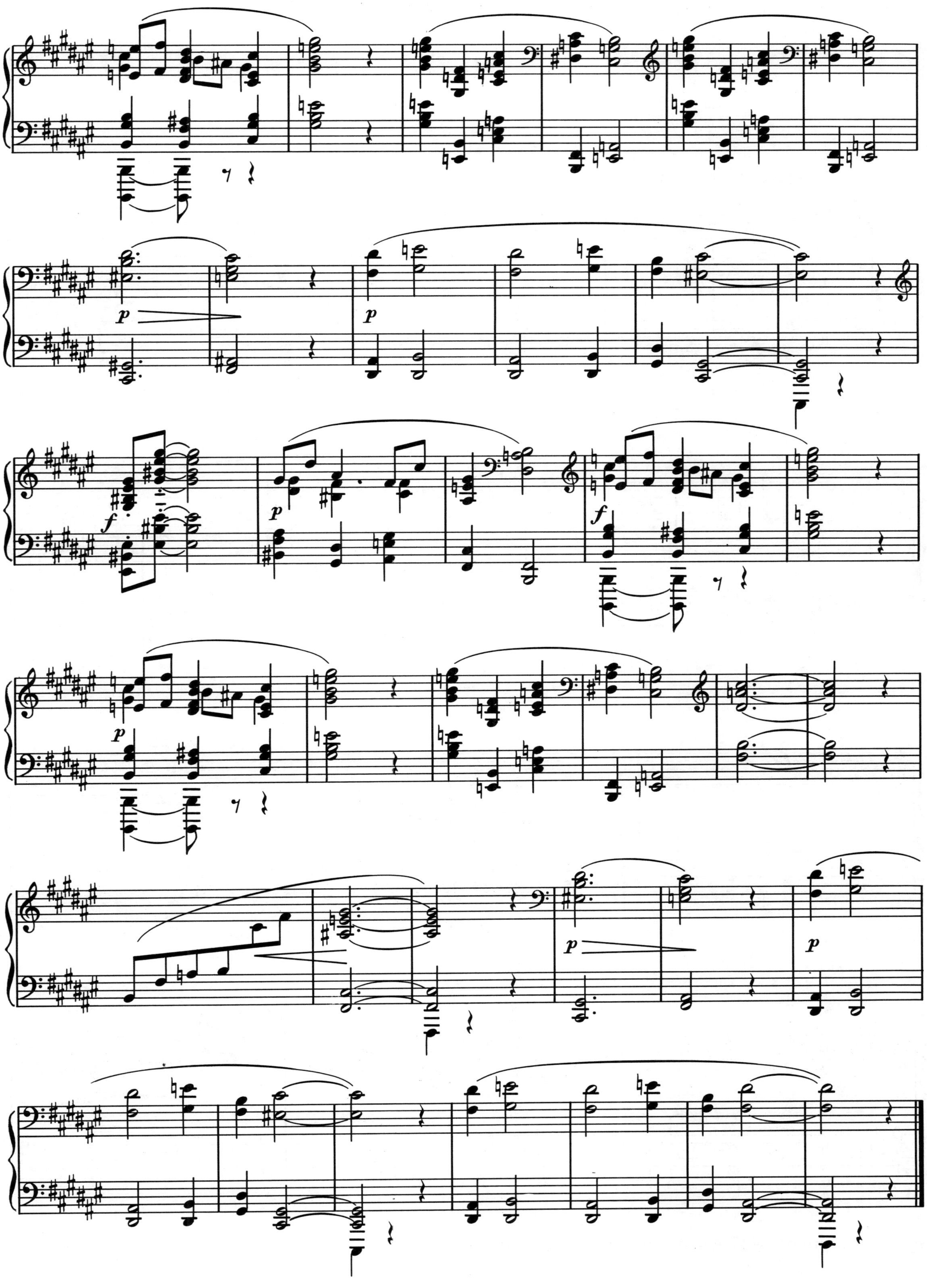
p
p
f
p
f
p
p
p

Sarabande

(1887)

No. III

Erik Satie

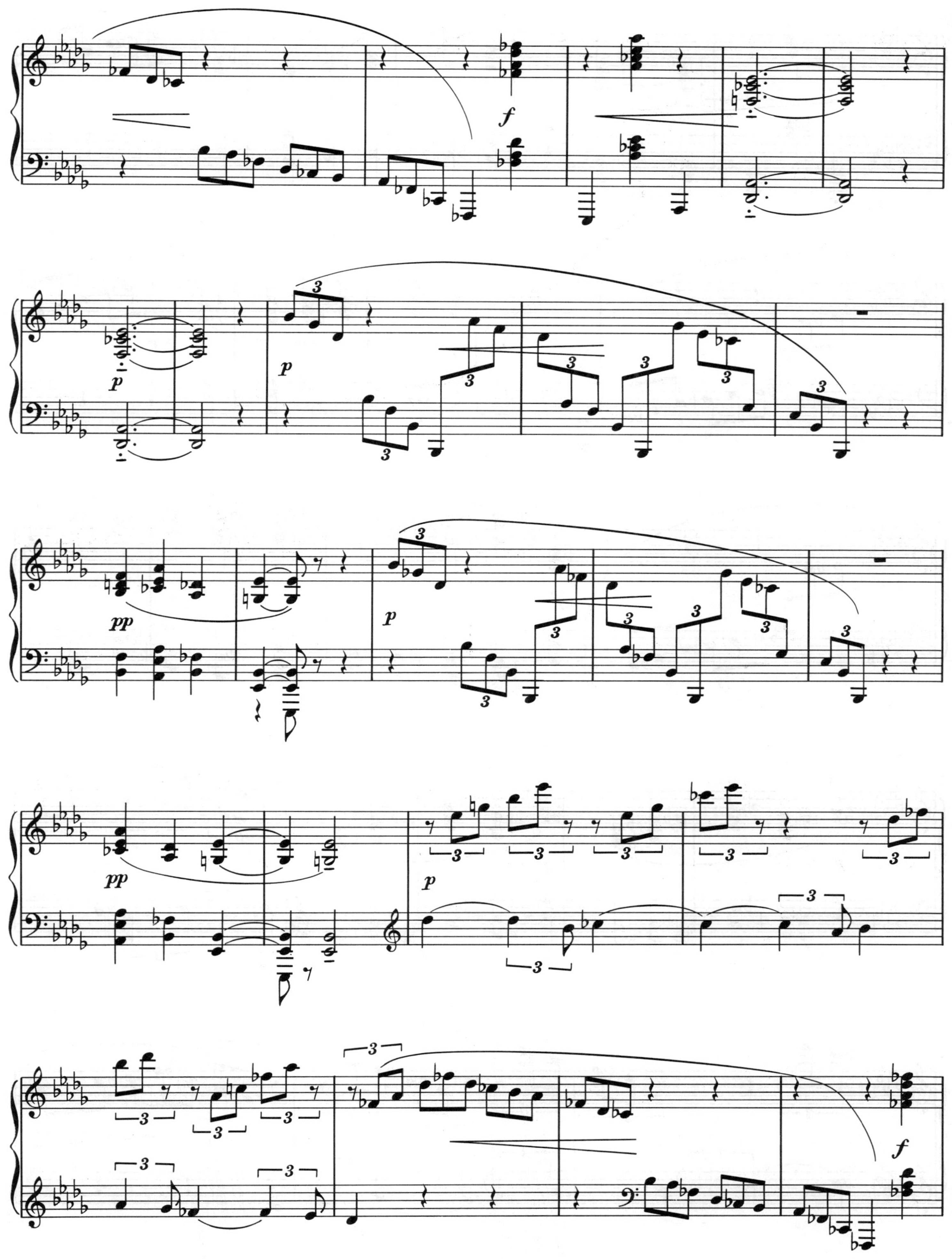
f
p
p
pp
p
pp
p
f

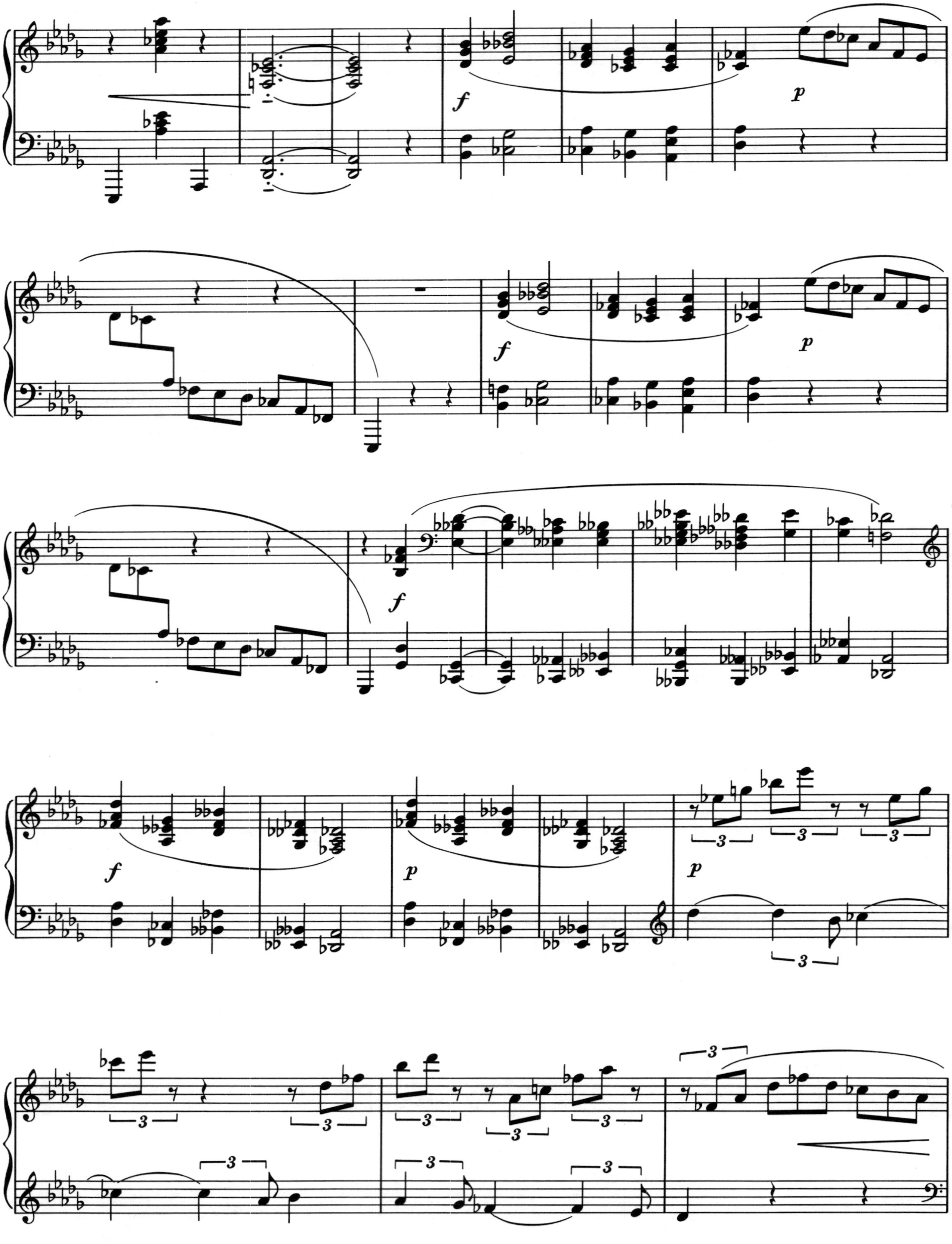
f
p
f
p
f
f
p
p
3

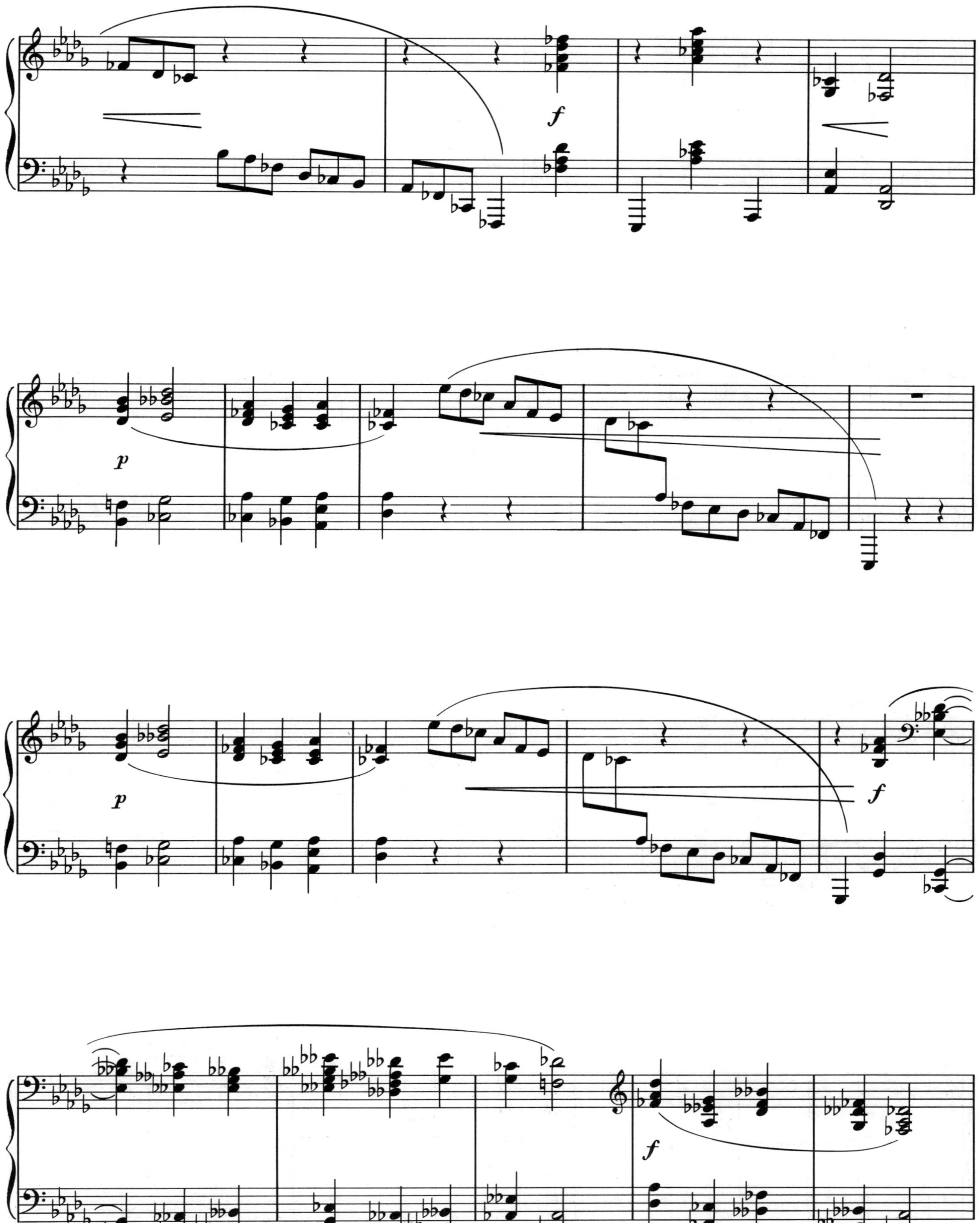
f
p
p
f
f

A.P. 10987654321